How To Be A
BLACK ENTREPRENEUR
In
The Age Of Connectivity

By

**Bro. Bedford
Host of Conversations With Black
Millionaire Entrepreneurs**

How to Be a Black Entrepreneur in the Age of Connectivity

By BROTHER BEDFORD
© Copyright 2014 Global Marketing & Publishing LLC.
All Rights Reserved.

No part of this publication may be reproduced or transmitted in any form whatsoever, electronic, or mechanical, including photocopying, recording, or by any informational storage or retrieval system without permission in writing from the author or publisher, (except by a reviewer who may quote brief passages in a review).

DISCLAIMER AND/OR LEGAL NOTICES:

The Publisher and Author make no representations or warranties with respect to the accuracy or completeness of the contents of this work and specifically disclaim all warranties, including without limitation warranties of fitness for a particular purpose. No warranty may be created or extended by sales and promotional materials. The advice and strategies contained herein may not be suitable for every situation. This work is sold with the understanding that the Publisher is not engaged in rendering legal, accounting, or other professional services. If advice concerning legal or related matters is needed, the services of a fully qualified professional should be sought. Neither the Publisher nor the Author shall be liable for damages arising here from. This publication is not intended for use as a source of legal or accounting advice. You should be aware of any laws, which govern business transactions or other business practices in your country and state. The information presented in this publication represents the view of the author as of the date of publication. Because of the rate with which conditions change, the author reserves the right to alter and update his opinion based on the new conditions. This publication is for informational purposes only. Any slights of people or organizations are unintentional.. Any reference to any person or business whether living or dead is purely coincidental.

Cover Design and layout by Anthony Stewart ~ www.anthonystewart.net

Also by Bro. Bedford:
The series- **Conversations with Black Millionaire Entrepreneurs: No-Nonsense Lessons from Those Who've Been There, Done That!**

Meet Bro. Bedford online and receive free training at:
www.brobedford.com

DEDICATED to my mother, Mary Ann Estes-Crenshaw, who has been a rock and constant support of the ambitions and desires for me, my siblings, and all of her grandchildren no matter what they are.

DEDICATED to all of my brothers and sisters, nieces and nephews who are always there when I need them.

DEDICATED to all of the brothers and sisters I have encountered in the struggle to help Black People be what Almighty God wants us to be.

SPECIAL DEDICATION to my wife Meredith and our 6 children who love and support me and put up with me while I strive to grow and develop and realize my full potential.

Contents

Foreword by William R. Patterson Chairman and CEO of The Baron Solution Group

Introduction	7
Chapter 1: Old Economy	11
Chapter 2: Black America is Worse	17
Chapter 3: The New Economy	19
Chapter 4: The Age of Connectivity	21
Chapter 5: Why Black Entrepreneurship is So Important	23
Chapter 6: So You Want to Be An Entrepreneur	25
Chapter 7: Entrepreneurial Commitment	27
Chapter 8: Thinking Like an Entrepreneur	33
Chapter 9: The Life Blood of an Entrepreneur	37
Chapter 10: Entrepreneurs Must Make Decisions	41
Chapter 11: Abandoning Your Comfort Zone	49
Chapter 12: Hurdles to Entrepreneurial Success	51
Chapter 13: The Age of The Entrepreneur	61
Chapter 14: The World Has Changed	63
Chapter 15: The Technological Edge	69
Chapter 16: Entrepreneurs in The Age of Connectivity	73
Chapter 17: The Key to Success in The Age of Connectivity	79
Chapter 18: The Most Important Skill in The Age Of Connectivity	83
Chapter 19: Entrepreneurs Take Action	87
Chapter 20: Closing thoughts	89

Foreword by
William R. Patterson
Chairman and CEO
The Baron Solution Group

*"Watch your thoughts, they become words;
watch your words, they become actions;
watch your actions, they become habits;
watch your habits, they become character;
watch your character, for it becomes your destiny."*
— **Frank Outlaw**
Late President of the Bi-Lo Stores

In the following pages of this book, you will learn from Brother Bedford a powerful mindset and approach that many of the most successful entrepreneurs have used to build thriving businesses. If you desire to change your destiny and create a legacy that you can be proud of for your family and the world, leverage Brother Bedford's insights to develop the thinking, words and behavior that can propel you to the ranks of the most successful entrepreneurs.

I am truly excited to see what you will be motivated to create after reading this book because as Brother Bedford states, there has never been a better time to be an entrepreneur. Everything is at your fingertips, and answers to nearly every problem can be found online. If you need money to grow your business, you can do an internet search for "Top Ways to Finance Your Business," and in less than a second find countless relevant search results.

If you need customers for your business, you can do a search for "Top Ways to Get Customers." You will easily find videos, audios, articles, podcasts, blogs, websites, communities and coaches dedicated to the topic. Anything that you want to know how to do and the best ways to address any problem can now be found online. Therefore, the "I'm stuck, and I don't know what to do," excuse is no longer valid. We have the Information Age to thank for this incredible level of access to the education and resources that we need.

Today is a new day! The Information Age and Digital Economy have now evolved into the Connected Age. This evolution includes huge mega trends such as lifestyle branding, social, mobile, local, collaboration, online communities, crowdfunding, microjob sites, video marketing and conferencing, mass personalization, and on-demand fulfillment of products and services.

Every time there is an evolutionary shift, it is as though a wealth reset button is pressed. The perceptive few who anticipate these shifts and position themselves to capitalize on the related trends will not only profit, but often dominate their markets due to first mover advantage.

Because of this wealth reset concept, I have often said that the answer to income and wealth mobility for Black America will not be found through the corporate job market but through entrepreneurship. These evolutionary megatrends present Black entrepreneurs with an unprecedented opportunity to increase their income and build wealth.

At The Baron Solution Group, we teach that there are four keys to accelerated wealth building: owning and leveraging your time; doing the things that the wealthiest and most successful people do; operating in arenas where there is no limit to the amount of money that you can make; and growing relationships with key influencers and decision makers.

As a child growing up, I had two big dreams. One was

to be a professional basketball player. The other dream was to be the CEO of a Fortune 100 company. When it came to my basketball dream, people would always say to me, "Are you crazy? You're more likely to be struck by lightning than to make it into the NBA." And they meant that literally. The odds of being struck by lightning are 1 in 700,000. The odds of making it into the NBA are 1 in 1,000,000.

Despite my valiant attempts and 250 free throws at 5:30 every morning in the park, I broke my hand during college recruiting and had to give up on my basketball dream. After that unfortunate event, I turned my attention to my other big dream, becoming a Fortune 100 CEO. When I thought about my goal, I had a nice chuckle knowing my naysayers probably thought I had a better chance of making it into the NBA.

My uncle once said to me, "People don't pay you to work for them. They pay you not to work for yourself. Own your time!" At that point, I knew I had to become an entrepreneur. I understood the power of having control of the 40-70 hours a week that I might spend working for someone else and, instead, directing that time and energy toward my own billion-dollar idea. It is because I own and leverage my time that I'm now able to run a successful financial holding company with subsidiaries, over 30 Web businesses, and The Baron Solution Group, which I grew from a $19.95 book into one of the top 100 women and minority businesses in the mid-atlantic region.

I remember once being asked in an interview, "As a wealth and business coach, what is your definition of wealth?" I replied, "The ability to perceive a market opportunity and then bring structure to an idea to capitalize on that opportunity ... Money comes and goes, but when you develop the skill to perceive opportunities and structure businesses around those opportunities, it's like having a license to print money. That's true wealth. That's being a Baron."

To those few individuals who may be reading this Foreword and are saying, "That sounds great, but it won't work for me because ...," I have a business coaching client named Christopher E. Powell who is able to run two successful online companies despite having cerebral palsy and limited use of his arms and hands. Chris once told me, "People are often shocked at all the things that I'm able to do when they learn I have cerebral palsy. I always tell them, don't be surprised.

The greatest disability is not from the neck down, it is from the neck up. Your mindset is everything." I also have clients who have mental disabilities and despite the associated challenges, they are able to run successful businesses online and offline. They don't make excuses when it comes to success, and after reading this book, neither should you.

I want to make one final point about Black entrepreneurship. I'm a big proponent of Black business, but to me, Black business does not just mean Black people buying the products and services of Black owned businesses. It means everyone buying Black. There are over one billion people in China, but Chinese entrepreneurs don't just sell products to the Chinese market. They sell goods and services internationally.

In my opinion, Black entrepreneurs should strive to do the same. To tap into diverse local, national, and global markets, Black entrepreneurs must learn to increase their capacity to deliver greater value in the marketplace.

An important point to keep in mind is that people don't buy Black, they buy value. Value comes in many forms including price, quality, accessibility, reliability, support, aesthetics, perceived elevation of status, and overall customer experience. So, use this bookt to enhance your thinking and to increase your capacity to profit by delivering higher value in the global marketplace.

To the Black entrepreneur: now is your time! This is your moment. Leverage it to do something great.

Introduction

Thank you for taking the time out to read what I hope is the most no-nonsense, straight to the point, and blunt book you've read about being and succeeding as a" **Black Entrepreneur".**

This information is not about classroom theory. I learned a few years ago that you couldn't eat theory. You can't pay your bills with theory.

What I share in these next few pages is from my over 15 years in business. The first phase of my entrepreneurial journey was in the entertainment arena on the artist side and then in promotions of Concerts and comedy shows.

The second phase of my journey was in the Real Estate arena where between 1999 and 2004 I participated in over $2 Million of Real Estate transactions that included raising private capital, buying and selling residential property.

Since 2005 up until the present my operations have shifted to the Internet where I've been building a **"Portable Digital Empire"** teaching **'Entrepreneurship'** and **'Online Business Building'**.

Mind you I have made some serious mistakes along the way, but I have also had some sweet successes.

My greatest insight into entrepreneurship has been reflecting on my past experiences and extensive study, but also my in depth **'Conversations With Black Millionaire Entrepreneurs'**! Those interviews can be accessed at http://www.conversationswithblackmillionaires.com

I try to distill some of that information to you in these pages.

If you are one of my fellow entrepreneurs with a business already you may find yourself nodding your head and saying to yourself, *"this brother feels me"*.

And you may find comfort in knowing that you are not alone in the world of entrepreneurship.

If you are thinking about becoming an entrepreneur in this '***Age of Connectivity***' this reporting might scare you away. If it does, know that the entrepreneurial arena is not for you. The new economy is not a place for the easily worried or intimidated.

If you continue on the entrepreneurial trek, I Hope and Pray that this reporting will help you avoid some of the pitfalls and problems that would normally come up and deal with those issues that cannot be avoided.

What will be shared in the rest of these pages will not be your traditional basics of business or how to start a business. There are plenty of works available dealing with that.

What I want to do is help you move forward boldly and more confidently into a new emerging reality. This is about going after success in this era, '***The Age of Connectivity***'.

So before we get into '**What**' it's going to take and '**How**' to achieve it we should get clear on what we're actually dealing with…

Chapter 1

The Old Economy

"Turn out the lights, the party's over. They say that all good things must end". Those were the words from an old Willie Nelson song and they seem appropriate with what has taken place in the economy over the last few years.

The party has ended.

What we have witnessed over the last few years is the painful unveiling of extreme and systemic weakness. All of the flaws and vulnerabilities have been made manifest.

All of the symptoms were present, but like a patient in denial the American public continued to participate in the activities that led to the economy being diseased in the first place.

You may ask what activities?

Overcapacity of Stores

It was hard to drive a couple of blocks and not run into the same store you saw in the last block. It got so bad at one point that there was a reporting of Starbucks opening up a new Starbucks location in the rest room of an existing Starbucks. **WOW!**

Home Depot and Lowe's became the border for every major city. They became the staple of every new housing development. Did I say staple as in Staples and Office

Depot, they began to spring up just like the home improvement stores.

There were literally thousands of restaurants across the street from each other selling the same menu items at the same prices.

You could drive into shopping plazas all across America and have the choice of a CVS, Rite Aid, and Walgreens right next door to each other.

The marketplace just couldn't support this overcapacity of stores forever. It was only a matter of time before the support collapsed.

Brands Lost Their Brand

Look at how some of the automakers had to close down whole brands. Let's use GM as an example.

A company like GM sold Cadillac, Buick, GMC, Pontiac, Saturn, Saab, and Hummer. Anyone with an eye could see that some of the vehicles were the same and overlapped, with different names.

GM sold pickup trucks by Chevy and GMC not to mention Cadillac. Talk about competing with yourself. GM was not alone in this practice of having overlapping brands.

If we go back and take a look at Starbucks we will see that they started selling cheese and egg breakfast sandwiches, while McDonalds started selling lattes.

Submarine shops started selling Pizza and Pizza shops started selling sub sandwiches. Brands have become blurred and so it is harder to identify who is who and what is what. What a mess!!!

Too Much Stuff

It seemed for awhile that everyone had two or three cars. Everyone had flat screen TVs, and multiple computers. It seemed that people were getting their houses remodeled every six months.

There is only so much a consumer can consume before they need a break to digest what they've already consumed.

Easy Credit

Many will argue that it was the access to easy credit and money that led to a lot of the excesses that we've already touched on.

In some areas of the country home values tripled in value allowing people to feel that their wealth increased and they started using their homes as an ATM machine, thus fueling over consumption.

Once the true value of these properties were realized, people began to see that they were underwater, meaning they owed more on their properties than what they were truly worth.

This brought reckless consumption to a halt, removing the support that all of the retail stores enjoyed during the so-called "boom". This point goes back to our earlier section dealing with the over capacity of stores.

The flip side of easy credit is the financial crisis that griped the entire banking sector. The issuing of mortgages based on inflated equity with not much attention being given to the ability of repayment was one of the major problems that initiated the crumbling of the old economy.

These instruments were bundled together into exotic investment packages and spread throughout the earth like a virus. This led to the exposure of the fragility of some of the world's major financial institutions.

Some of the companies that were apart of this practice, Bear Stearns, Lehman Brothers, Merrill Lynch, and Countrywide Financial **don't even exist anymore**.

We could go on and on discussing the many activities that have led to the unraveling of the economy, but that would take us far away from the scope of this book.

However, there is another important point we need to discuss that has been impacted by the implosion of the Old Economy.

JOBS! JOBS! JOBS!

This has become the battle cry of the country. Since 2007 over **5 million jobs have been lost**. As I write this the reported current unemployment rate is hovering around 7%. The ***"unofficial unemployment rate"*** is over **14%**.

Over 20% of the U.S. workforce is underemployed, according to the Gallup daily tracking. The underemployed are people who have jobs that do not fully occupy them and so they do not earn sufficient wages to properly cover their needs.

This is a huge problem brewing in America.

Where Oh Where Has the Middle Class Gone

The disappearance of old-style manufacturing jobs has been a severe blow to middle class America.

According to Bloomberg News, many of the jobs lost will **NEVER** return.

This has created an environment where former low-skilled factory workers are competing with high school and college graduates for jobs that pay minimum wage or slightly better.

If we factor in the elderly vying for those same jobs, because their retirement doesn't look as secure as it once looked, we have the worst employment environment since the Great Depression.

Chapter 2

Black America Is Worse

I've given you a few views as to what has led to the unraveling of the economy and its impact on the employment picture in America.

It is even more disturbing to know that as bad as the numbers are; Black People are doing far worse in **ALL** areas.

The unemployment picture for Black People is double the National average. In some areas the unemployment rates are triple and quadruple that of whites.

If we dig deeper and focus on just Black Males the numbers get crazy and don't seem real approaching 50% in some urban areas.

The National Urban League released its annual report titled, *The State of Black America*. The report measures disparities between blacks and whites in economics, education, health, civic engagement and social justice.

Marc Morial, president and CEO of the National Urban League, said, "As we examine the State of Black America…, ***we are overwhelmed by the current crisis of unemployment."***

The emphasis is mine.

So to sum up this section I believe it is safe to say that

the economy that you once knew is **DEAD**. It is not coming back to life either.

Now some would look at this as negative, but throughout history whenever a major change took place those at the forefront of that change benefited greatly.

Napoleon Hill said, ***"Every adversity carries within it the seed of equal or greater benefit."***

As bad as the adversity is that we must deal with in the crumbling 'Old Economy', the seed for entrepreneurial greatness in the 'New Economy' is present.

So let's move on and talk about the 'New Economy' and **WHY** the need for Black Entrepreneurship is so, so important for the future of Black America.

Chapter 3

The New Economy

The New Economy is presenting us with '*New Realities*' and '*New Opportunities*'. Never before in history has someone been able to startup and grow a business so fast. The new uses of media and technology make it possible for anyone.

Not to mention that all of the barriers that prevented us from reaching into certain marketplaces have vanished.

But I must be frank, along with the ease that the 'New Economy' presents comes a higher level of pressure. **Crisis and problems will come faster and more intense**. Your entrepreneurial success will come from your ability to handle and navigate through the pressure cooker.

Mental and Emotional toughness are pre-requisites for the entrepreneur in this new era of business. (I'll touch on this later)

The New Age Economy will be tougher and more demanding and here's why:

The Custom is back in Customer

The power has shifted back to the customer. There is zero tolerance for inferior products or services. So customers will not just be spending money for the sake of spending money.

Customers will be more scrutinizing of the businesses they support. Businesses will have to have superior _expert positioning_ and _high value propositions_ to appeal to customers. Your reputation must say a whole lot about you before you are even considered for business.

Customers will be striving to be more responsible and cautious with their spending. Think about it, aren't you attempting to be a little more cautious and responsible consumer. This applies to your potential customers as well.

In the Age of Connectivity entrepreneurs must earn the right to the customer's attention. They are not just going on buying frenzies, buying whatever it is you have to offer. You have to provide specialized, maybe even customized products and services.

People now have the power and they are aware that they have the opportunity to demand specifically what they want and need.

The bottom line is that entrepreneurs must be more **customer-centered, smarter, more strategic in their thinking and more creative** if they are to survive and thrive in the 'Age of Connectivity'.

Chapter 4

The Age of Connectivity

Before I explain why entrepreneurship is vital to the African American community and re-enforce your decision to pursue entrepreneurship, as well as, give you some tips and strategies on what you can do to ensure your success, I should clarify what the 'Age of Connectivity' is.

There are over **2 Billion connected computers** in the world.

There are over **6.5 Billion mobile connections** worldwide. And those numbers are expected to more than double by the end of 2015.

You can record on a smartphone and with the press of a button **communicate with over 80% of the world's population basically for free**.

The smartphones have built-in HD cameras, that's like having a portable studio in your hand. Press record and broadcast all over the world. **You can publish on YouTube and have your own TV channel.**

You can have a book published and distributed on Amazon in 48 hours. You don't even need a traditional publisher to release a book today.

You can have a multi-media product made from information online and making money in less than 24 hours.

Distribution is not what it used to be. <u>You and I are in control of the media.</u> The traditional "big boys" are becoming obsolete, **anyone can broadcast a message and deliver a product and you don't need permission.**

When you understand how distribution works today and with the reach of social media channels combined with the simple production I mentioned above, you realize the old barriers no longer exist.

They're gone!

It is possible to build relationships and do business with virtually anyone on the planet. To bring your idea and message to life today, all it takes is the right mindset, the right kind of education and training, the right tools, and a little effort.

I hope to share these things in the following pages.

Chapter 5

Why Black Entrepreneurship Is Soooo Important!

I have spent almost all of my life as an entrepreneur, the last 6+ years as a consultant, coach, and advisor to entrepreneurs. I consider myself an advocate for 'Black Entrepreneurs'.

Choosing to be an entrepreneur takes a lot of courage by itself, but understanding the overall impact of entrepreneurs on their communities is very significant.

It is the entrepreneurs that create the majority of jobs, products, and services that make family and home life enjoyable.

It is the entrepreneurs that help create the environment to make life more rewarding and interesting.

It is the successful entrepreneurs that provide investment capital for medical research and new technology.

It is the successful entrepreneurs that turn dilapidated and blighted areas into vibrant livable and safe communities.

The support for hospitals and medical centers, libraries and museums, educational institutions and charities come from concerned and involved entrepreneurs.

So when you look at the black community and it is void of these critical elements that provide health and life, then know that the need to cultivate and grow black entrepreneurs is not an option.

Black Entrepreneurship is more important in the 'Age of Connectivity' than any time in our history.

Chapter 6

So You Want To Be An Entrepreneur

I hope to help you see that the time has never been better to be an Entrepreneur and the tools that can make you a phenomenal success have never been more accessible, however, it is important to understand the Real Deal about Entrepreneurship.

Many people including textbook "gurus" make the assertion that you need to have the best product/service, a ton of capital, the smartest lawyer to be successful as an Entrepreneur.

And on the other hand having the worst product/service, no money and a mediocre lawyer does not mean failure as an Entrepreneur.

I have witnessed people with no apparent resources and horrible conditions succeed. And I have seen people with everything going for them still fail and make a mess.

The truth is there is no such thing as a business failure or success; *you have people successes and people failures.*

If you are to be successful as an Entrepreneur you cannot be reactive. You must be **proactive**, **assertive**, and **creative** in making decisions and make things happen.

This can be very difficult for someone who has entered the entrepreneurial arena by default. Meaning they became an entrepreneur because they disliked their job or they were frustrated with their manager or supervisor or maybe they were forced into early retirement.

The employee who turned entrepreneur because of default or frustration brings to the entrepreneurial arena a lot of mental and emotional baggage.

The **behavior**, **habits**, and **attitudes** that work in the workplace just don't work in the entrepreneurial environment. And this is the major reason that so many budding entrepreneurs fail.

If you truly want to succeed as an entrepreneur you must let go of anchors that have worked well in your previous environment but are diametrically opposed to Entrepreneurial Life.

Chapter 7

Entrepreneurial Commitment

I happen to be present when **Billionaire Bob Johnson** answered a question from a gentleman who asked, *"What do you think about people working their jobs and looking into home based business opportunities on the side?"*

Bob Johnson said, *"I don't give to much energy to people who are trying to be entrepreneurs."* Some took offense to what he said, but I understood it.

He was saying that you can't half way *try* to be an entrepreneur. You are going to have to be very committed to the process of entrepreneurship.

Now I'm not saying that you shouldn't keep your job and build your business on the side, in fact I recommend that for some people.

Bob Johnson was speaking of his entrepreneurial journey and the commitment it took for him to have success.

Many of the successful entrepreneurs that I have had the honor of interviewing and working with had to sleep in cars or on floors and cook on hot plates before they succeeded in certain areas.

And if they were just half heartedly trying or just kickin' the tires they would have given up and quit. Simply trying leaves you open to certain people, attitudes, behaviors, and habits.

The _attitude_, _behavior_, and _habits_ of an entrepreneur are completely different from most people you know. People that are fearful, doubtful, and not supportive of your ambitions should occupy only a small portion of your time.

As disciplined as I think I am and as much as I pride myself on being a strong minded person, my resilience and performance are impacted by…

> *What I'm reading,*
> *What I'm listening to, and*
> *Who I'm hanging around*

This is why I advise entrepreneurs to develop mastermind groups and seek out coaches or mentors.

Am I saying that you can't socialize with family and friends who are not entrepreneurial? Of course I'm not.

I am simply stating that to protect you or balance out negative and anti-business thinking you must immerse yourself in groups that are in line with your goals and desires.

You can really expedite your entrepreneurial success and diminish your isolation related stress by associating with other progressive entrepreneurs.

Because, before you get to where you want to be as an entrepreneur you may have to suffer a lot, including being embarrassed and stressed out.

And it helps that you are connected with other committed entrepreneurs who can help you.

You Work Too Much

You are going to discover that most people, who are not entrepreneurs, will become frustrated with you. And you will also find that they have hardened biases against you.

When I spoke with the wonderful **Cathy Hughes of Radio and TV One**, she mentioned how when she was starting her business one of the things she had to deal with was people telling her to get a life.

They asked her if she was sacrificing too much of her time and energy attending to her business. She had to finally tell people '*her business was her life.*'

The truth is for a bona fide entrepreneur the line between work and play is blurred.

And most times your commitment to your business life will cause tension, annoyance, and confusion for those around you.

Many will say that you don't love your spouse or significant other. You will be accused of neglecting responsibilities that are not related to work. **You will become known as the workaholic.**

In truth, most entrepreneurs may be happier and more in touch with reality than their critics.

The critics are usually tied into dead end jobs doing things they find boring and unfulfilling, and they can't seem to harness enough gumption to do anything about it.

So your critics will label you a workaholic because they resent their own *"stagnation in life"* and they make themselves feel better by making you feel guilty.

Now here's something for you to ponder. As entrepreneurs we must resist the urge to label all our critics as jealous, unreasonable, or just plain haters. (Smile)

The reality is we are just coming from two completely different modes of thinking.

The deeper point that I'm making is that we pose a special problem for others and the more we understand that the more creative we can be at **striking a balance** between loved ones and work.

Believe me, you need both.

YOU ARE A GAMBLER

Another perception that your loved ones may have about you choosing to be an entrepreneur is that you are a wild-eyed risk taker.

It has always struck me as kind of funny that in this society when we depart from a friend or a loved one we say *"be careful"*. We don't say, *"Be happy"* or *"be successful"*.

Not that you shouldn't be careful, but the norm is to push the side of caution instead of 'risk'. And to be successful as an entrepreneur you must embrace risk. Without risk there is no progress.

History shows us that the most successful people always throw caution to the wind to some degree.

Running a business does carry a degree of risk, but it doesn't have to be foolish.

Anxiety about the risk that come along with business is natural. The objective of the entrepreneur is to manage risk, not take unnecessary risk.

YOU'RE THE ONE

The truth is when you decide to be an entrepreneur; you're deciding to take your life and future into your own hands. You're deciding to be autonomous.

To succeed as an entrepreneur, you are setting aside the neediness of acceptance from others. You must become immune to criticism, because as you move forward in your endeavors, criticism will come.

When you join the ranks of entrepreneurs you'll have to start accepting **100%** responsibility for your success. **Make no excuses!**

Entrepreneurial success requires a strong sense of autonomy. The mental toughness that you must develop will put you in a good position to handle things when your business hits some rough spots, and it will.

One sad part about business is that you very rarely end up with the people you start with. There are many reasons that people will come and go.

You will outgrow some of your partners, associates, employees and friends. Some will begin to resent you, and yes some will become jealous.

The truth about entrepreneurship is _business can't be run by committee_, the buck stops with you.

That may not be fun. But it's the truth. **You're the one.**

Chapter 8

Thinking Like an Entrepreneur

All my life I have had the desire to be in business for myself. I have only had probably three jobs in my life and maybe one lasted longer than 60 days.

From my late teens onward I have worked for myself. I started in the Entertainment Industry, first as a performer then as a promoter. I had some successes, but I also had some serious Disasters.

After a few years of serious trial and error I began to Study more about business and ask a lot of questions from those who appeared to be successful. In my quest I stumbled on to Real Estate and I was hooked.

I started however like many people buying, fixing, renting, and **crying**☺…many of you landlords know what I mean.

As I continued to expand on my education I came across a technique that was completely different from what I was accustomed to. In fact everyone I tried to share it with thought I was crazy, however, **I persisted and my first transaction netted me $6,000.**

I was so nervous after I received the check I went straight to the bank to cash it…to see if it was real.

I took the money home and put it in my mattress for two weeks. I just knew that someone was going to come knocking on my door and take the money or worse the police were going to arrest me for doing the deal. Guess what... no one ever came.

In fact when I saw the gentleman that I sold the house to one day I just knew he was going to come up to me and demand his money back. Instead he told me to call him when I got another deal like that one.

At that moment an Entrepreneur was born. I realized that every thing I thought I knew about business was wrong. Everything my friends said was wrong.

Everything my family said was wrong. In fact everything I had learned in school and what I thought I knew about money and business was wrong...**DEAD WRONG.**

At that moment I realized Entrepreneurs think differently than everybody else.

The term Entrepreneur is a French term for a **person, who undertakes,** in a capitalist society you can add to that definition *a person who undertakes and develops a new enterprise at some risk (of failure or loss).*

Although the words innovator, proprietor, and capitalist are used in the same sense, there are subtle differences that make the term "entrepreneur" preferable.
The Idea for the undertaking may not be the entrepreneur's own invention, he or she is not simply an owner of the business and the capital raised for it may or may not be his/her own.

Most people that you know work for someone else and are dependent on others for their livelihood and security.

Entrepreneurs, on the other hand, choose to think for

themselves and run their own business for the sake of financial and personal independence.
INDEPENDENCE is the deep-rooted motivator of all entrepreneurs.

Ultimately the key to your personal independence is your mind. Becoming a successful entrepreneur allows you the ultimate freedom, freedom of your own thoughts.

The independence of your own thinking is the only real source from which all other forms of independence flow.

Entrepreneurs are made and born. Anyone can become one. There is no secret formula or magic touch. Prosperous entrepreneurs come in every size, shape, and personality.

There is only one common denominator: *entrepreneurs presented with the same information as others see things other people do not see.*

THE LANGUAGE OF AN ENTREPRNEUR

This next aspect of entrepreneurship is often overlooked, but it is just as important as any other element. **It is important to master the language of an entrepreneur**. Just like any industry or discipline, business has its own language.

When you listen to a doctor speak to other doctors he speaks the language of doctors. When lawyers speak to other lawyers they speak the language of lawyers.

Whatever field you choose to go into you must speak the language of that field. If you want to be successful in the world of business/entrepreneurship you must work to master the language of business.

There is a saying, *"when you open your mouth to speak, you show the world what's on your mind."* You can tell what we are thinking by the words that come out of our mouths.

If we want people to know that we are about "our business", we must learn the vocabulary of business.

Thinking like an entrepreneur means expanding your vocabulary and training your mind in specific ways that protect your independence and ensure that you will continue on your journey to victory.

Chapter 9

The Lifeblood of an Entrepreneur

INFORMATION

Entrepreneurs make money with information and energy. Entrepreneurs make money with their minds.

The popular notion is that entrepreneurs are strong willed men and women of action. The truth is that entrepreneurs are strong-willed men and women but **first, of thought, and then of action.**

Their primary everyday action is thinking and relentlessly seeking information to allow them to continually give their customers, employees, and suppliers what they need (require) and want (desire) and get what they want in return, *"fair exchange-no robbery."*

Information--having it and knowing how to use it-is the key to business strength. Information is the great equalizer. It doesn't choose who receives it. Male or female, Black or white, Muslim or Christian, information has no bias.

Simply, <u>*information is a single fact. It is anything you see, hear, read, touch, talk about, sniff, observe, or question. It can be a word, a symbol, number, color, or comparison.*</u>

Information is the raw material for your thinking. Your mind gathers information with your five senses: **smell, sight, hearing, taste,** and **touch**. Information is anything that enters your mind.

A continual flow of new information is the only way you keep a pulse on the **New Economy**, your business, set priorities, prepare for and anticipate the future.

You think about it all, and use that information to make decisions and then take action.

Regardless to what industry or business you choose, **the key to your success will be how well you handle information**. You need to understand what information is, what information you need, where to get it, and how to use it.

From the very first day you must begin to acquire all the information you can about every aspect of your business or you won't make it. Nothing is more important.

If you are going to own a business for the very first time, you must prepare yourself to go through a revolution within yourself as you stretch your mind and develop skills, methods, and experience at gathering and thinking about information that is relevant to your business.

This means sorting, analyzing, dissecting, interpreting, reflecting on, organizing, questioning, and deciding on a whole lot of new information.

You will begin to deal with greater and more comprehensive information than ever before.

And you will have to do this everyday. It should become automatic, just like brushing your teeth in the morning, except you will do it all day, everyday.

The better and faster you get at gathering and thinking about new information the easier and more natural it will become. It's exercise for the mind; you will begin to love it.

WHERE TO GET INFORMATION

Last point on information, you must be extremely careful where you get your information. <u>Gathering information from the wrong sources can be dangerous</u>.

Always seek information from people who have expertise in the field that you are going into. Be careful of who you let into your head. People are always willing to give free advice, and it probably is worth every penny.

Always seek advice from those who have been down the road before you and they have come through the ups and downs to give you their experiences.

As an entrepreneur you should always read the business section of your local newspaper or its digital equivalent. Learn to seek information in all the regular places.

Every industry has its traditional sources of information: trade organizations, trade shows, trade publications and magazines, business magazines, (**Black Enterprise, Entrepreneur, Inc. Business Week**), consumer magazines (**Time, Newsweek, World report**), The New York Times Business section, Wall Street Journal, CNN, CNBC, Workshops, Seminars, books and Tapes.

All of these sources and others can be accessed online now with a simple search. The list is endless. The point is you have to become an information junkie. Your success will depend on you doing this very well.

And even when you become big enough to have someone gather information for you, no one will be able to use information and apply it in your business like you will.

Chapter 10

Entrepreneurs Must Make Decisions

In the last section I discussed the importance of information to an Entrepreneur, where to get it and how to use it. Information really is **The Lifeblood** of an Entrepreneur.

The ultimate purpose for gathering information about your business, customers, Employees, competition and everything that surrounds you is to prepare you for making decisions.

Your success as an Entrepreneur depends on you being able to take in relevant information and making the best decisions for you and your business on a continuous basis.

As an Entrepreneur you must train yourself to take vital and relevant information and create a knowledge base to make successful decisions.

The idea is not to make as many decisions as possible. **The idea is to make the right decisions.**

Three Levels of Decisions

I want to touch on the three levels of decisions. Some will probably say that there are more levels and more detailed and complex levels. And that may be true.

But my objective is to simplify the process for making decisions in your journey as an entrepreneur in the Age of Connectivity. That's it, nothing more.

The first level is surface decisions. Surface decisions are the most basic and obvious form. They are based on first impression…not much investigation.

Have you ever judged a book by its cover?

That's what surface decisions are. Never opening the book to read or understand its contents leaves you to prejudice, misinterpretation, and prejudgment.

This is not a good way to run your business or life, yet we make decisions like this everyday.

Now there is a way to get past surface decisions. **First,** you must remain patient and don't rush to make decisions that will impact your life, the life of your family, and others.

Next, open the book to get more information. This simply means to delve deeper into the information you gather to get a better understanding.

Finally, think about the information you just discovered. The more you think about pieces of information the clearer your perception of the information becomes.

The second level of making decisions is emotional decisions or as some like to call it *gut instinct*.

Gut instinct or emotional decisions carry more weight than surface decisions. These decisions are based on gathering more information and thinking more on the information.

Then you use <u>your instinct or your inner sense of knowing</u> the right thing to do then you make a decision. If you have been an entrepreneur for some time you understand exactly what I am saying.

When you are trying to satisfy customers in a new way or trying to improve on your customer service, product, distribution, marketing, you must go past the obvious. And in order to do this you keep gathering and thinking about information.

But you must have the courage to follow that inner voice, your instincts.

<u>That voice, your instincts is your inner business partner</u>. That partner will grow as you grow and will gain more experience as you do.

An emotional decision supported by more information, careful thought, and instinct, will always be much better than a surface decision.

However, there is a drawback to making emotional decisions.

The first and second levels of decision-making are not based purely on logic, and decisions are subject to change with more thought and new information.

<u>If you are missing critical information, your gut and emotional decisions can be wrong.</u>

Let me give you an example of what I am talking about.

I locked up a deal earlier in my Real Estate career from

HUD. It was a decent property and I really thought I was about to hit a nice lick. (Smile) I put down a $500 deposit and began to market the property.

I got some interested investors, but nobody came in with an offer that was sufficient to make a profit. My 30-day period was close to expiring and the Realtor talked me into giving HUD another $500 for an extension.

Now I have $1,000 in the deal. My gut and emotions were driving my decisions.

I fell short on gathering the appropriate information. **I offered too much for the property**. If I had continued to find out the true cost of repairs and what investors were paying for ugly houses in that area, I would have offered less for the property.

To make a long story short, I lost my $1,000.

The consequences of making emotional or gut decisions can be serious. In this above example I lost $1,000.

<u>The best part of the experience was I learned a whole lot. I did not die, I still have my first born, and the lessons learned have allowed me to do these types of deals quite easily today.</u>

But I don't think if I would have kept making those types of decisions I would be sharing this information with you. Those $1,000 losses could kill an entrepreneur very fast.

The great challenge for Black Entrepreneurs is to make sound, intelligent, and knowledgeable decisions time after time.

<u>The last and highest level of making decisions **is**</u>
KNOWLEDGE DECISIONS.

Decisions based on Knowledge come from having all of the important info and a vast amount of experience (**yours or someone else's**) so that you know what information you need, where to get it, and the type of questions to ask to validate the information.

These decisions are fully explainable, because they are based in logic. When you don't have to question anyone else or yourself as to whether or not you made the right decision, you've made a Knowledge decision.

When you don't have all of the necessary information, knowledge decisions are impossible. **That's why you must be patient.**

You have to continue to gather, to analyze, to think about, to question, and ponder over all the information, which is so critical to your success.

Now that you know that information is the lifeblood of an entrepreneur. You must set up a system to continue to get the information you need.

Let me give you another example, another Real Estate deal that I came across was similar to the deal I mentioned above.

However, this time instead of letting my emotions dictate the deal; I had my system/team in place to give me the information I needed.

I had an appraiser give me the true value of the property

after repairs. I had a contractor…ok handyman give me an estimate of repairs, and I had a Title Company give me a history of the property.

Therefore, when I made my offer and it was accepted, I knew I had a Slam Dunk!

When I began to market the property, two investors showed up at the property at the same time and began to make offers right there on the front porch, a bidding war right in front of me.

Needless to say I was as quiet as a church mouse… Slam Dunk!

It was such a Slam Dunk! That I made four times what I thought I would make on the deal. Why?

Because I had all the information I needed to make a **KNOWLEDGE DECISION** instead of an emotional decision.

As Entrepreneurs we must make conscious efforts to build our decision-making skills. And we must learn the art of patience. Knowledge decisions require *time, information*, and experience.

The better you get at gathering information and the more experience you gain the better your decisions will be.

Study your decisions. Analyze previous decisions. What worked and what didn't work? What would you have done different and what would you do the next time? Analyze the successful decisions as well as the unsuccessful. If you made right decisions, that's great. If not, correct them. One bad decision can really stall your momentum. You have complete responsibility for all your decisions.

Remember, "*all we are, is the sum total of the decisions we make*".

Chapter 11

Abandoning Your Comfort Zone

Everyone has a **COMFORT ZONE** in which they live and work. Your Comfort zone is determined by many factors and can be changed with practice and time.

You have a choice of how you spend your time, what you want to achieve and how much money you make… I'm going to say that last part again…**You Have a Choice on HOW MUCH MONEY YOU MAKE!**

This may come as a surprise to some one who is convinced their income is someone else's choice, not theirs, especially when the complete opposite is true.

Your income is the result of one thing and one thing only…

What You Choose To Do With Your Time

Here is what some have told me, "Bro. Bedford, you don't understand. I got a job. My boss tells me when to come to work and how much I can make. THEY tell me what my salary is."

I guess they are right. Someone else is definitely in control and will remain in control unless there is a major attitude change.

This book didn't just fall off of a shelf into your lap and I definitely did not spam you to draw your attention to it. You either subscribed to my list or you ordered this book from a reliable source, which means you know that there are opportunities available to you as an entrepreneur. You made a choice.

Many people are wrestling with the concept of having to exchange hours for dollars. Again, it boils down to what you are comfortable with.

How valuable is your time?

$8.00 an hour, $15.00 an hour, $25.00 an hour. *Your time is your most valued asset.*

What you determine to do with your time will determine the quality of your Life.

So I hope you are ready to expand your comfort zone. In fact in the 'Age of Connectivity' your comfort zone will be challenged often.

You have to get used to looking for and feeding on more information. The more time spent on gathering better information, the better you'll be able to make quality decisions. And the better the decisions, the better quality of life.

Chapter 12

Hurdles To Entrepreneurial Success

Even after you have made the decision to become an entrepreneur in this new era and you have began to continuously gather information and work to make the best decisions for you and your family, there are still many hurdles that you may face on the road to entrepreneurial success.

One of the main "Hurdles" to Entrepreneurial Success is…

FEAR

There are several types of fears or phobias that have a tremendous impact on how we pursue our lives and businesses. I want to touch on this first one because in my interaction with entrepreneurs or would be entrepreneurs I try to study what motivates us to become Entrepreneurs in the first place.

Instead of becoming an entrepreneur for personal and financial independence and freedom of your own thoughts and ideas, many become entrepreneurs out of Fear of Poverty.

This Fear of Poverty can manifest itself many ways that stops our success as Entrepreneurs. It kills ambition, imagination, enthusiasm, and it makes us mentally and physically lazy. This fear causes worry and anxiety.

This Fear also plants the seeds for other "habits" that

prohibit our success as Entrepreneurs.

Look at what Napoleon Hill writes in his classic book *Think & Grow Rich* about this most destructive hurdle,

"This fear paralyzes the faculty of reason, destroys the faculty of imagination, kills off self-reliance, undermines enthusiasm, discourages initiative, leads to uncertainty of purpose, encourages procrastination, wipes out enthusiasm and makes self-control an impossibility. It takes the charm from one's personality, destroys the possibility of accurate thinking, diverts concentration of effort; it masters persistence, turns the will-power into nothingness, destroys ambition, beclouds the memory and invites failure in every conceivable form; it kills love and assassinates the finer emotions of the heart, discourages friendship and invites disaster in a hundred forms, leads to sleeplessness, misery and unhappiness- and all this despite the obvious truth that we live in a world of over-abundance of everything the heart could desire, with nothing standing between us and our desires, excepting lack of a definite purpose"

As we can see Fear of Poverty should not be our motivation for what is actually a Human Right.

I once read that the acronym of F.E.A.R. means

False, Evidence, Appearing, Real

In order to kill fear we must equip ourselves with the knowledge that will do away with all the false evidence that has become the gigantic "Hurdles" to our Entrepreneurial Success.

The next 'Hurdle' to our Entrepreneurial Success is...

SELF DOUBT

All of us have doubts. *'I can't do that.'* *'I'm not smart like that.'* *'He or She is better than me.'*

Or we have family or friends who feel it is their duty to remind us of our imperfections, even when we don't ask.

They'll say things like, *'What makes you think you can do that?'* Or *'If your idea is so good, how come someone else hasn't done it yet.'*

Oh! This is a good one, ' *You don't know what you're talking 'bout. That'll never work.'*

These words get so **LOUD** in our heads and they create such a horrible feeling in our stomachs, that we become paralyzed. **We fail to move forward and we sit and watch Life pass us by.**

When we do this, we have embraced the noise and we crash into the 'Hurdle' of SELF DOUBT!

Proverb: *'That which you give attention to, grows in your Life'*

If you believe that you can't, you won't.

Owning your own business will always be someone else's reality and always your dream, if you follow this mindset.

In order to be a Successful Entrepreneur you must

develop the quality of **Positive Self-Expectancy.**

Even if no one else is positive about you...you **'MUST'** be positive about you.

I want to give you one of the things that I use to conquer *"SELF DOUBT."*

Set realistic goals. Write down the goals. Take action on the goals.
Once you set a goal and you take action on that goal, once it is accomplished you begin to remove SELF DOUBT, because you (the Self) are making something happen. Then you move on to the next goal.

I know this sounds easy, but who said this had to be hard. Let's find that person and give them a serious beat down for causing all this confusion.

When you see yourself jumping over the 'Hurdle' of SELF DOUBT, you'll see that the finish line is right around the bend.

It is important to take **ACTION** to overcome these "Hurdles". We don't want to still be standing at the starting line, while the race to success in the 'New Economy' is going on.

The next "Hurdle" to Entrepreneurial Success…

BAD HABITS

We see successful Entrepreneurs that appear to have it all together. They do the right things at the right time; they seem to say the most profound things. They are Peak

Performers.

Why are they like this? What gives them this wonderful appearance?

Most have developed Habits that lead to success, **Good Habits**.

It's like seeing a person that is in great shape. They are strong, they glow, and they are healthy and full of vitality.

We don't necessarily see the early morning workouts, the stringent diet that they have implemented in their life. We just know they look good. And we want to look just as good as they do if not better.

The Question becomes…Am I willing to get up an hour earlier to work out? Am I willing to push that German Chocolate Cake away from me? Am I willing to stop drinking and smoking?

Bad Habits have a tremendous gravitational pull-more than most of us realize or want to admit. They block our effectiveness and really stop us from achieving the Entrepreneurial Success we desire.

Just as breaking the Bad Habits of no exercise, bad diet, and bad lifestyle choices are difficult to break…so it is with the *Bad Habits of Procrastination* and the lack of discipline to "_read_" and "_study_". Which are those things we don't see successful Entrepreneurs doing… but they are!

The gravitational pull of some of our habits may be keeping us from going where we want to go. But if we replace those Bad Habits with Good Habits our Entrepreneurial Success is right at our fingertips.

FEAR, **SELF DOUBT**, **BAD HABITS** are all "Hurdles" that we must jump if we want to be successful as Entrepreneurs.

This next "Hurdle" comes up after we have decided to take the necessary steps to become successful and we begin to look for the tools we need to insure success.

You probably already know what this "Hurdle" is. Drum roll please…

LISTENING TO BAD ADVICE!

As we go through life, there will never be a shortage of people who want to give us advice. Parents, spouse, friends, in-laws, children,

they all have opinions about what you are doing with your business and what they think you should be doing.

In my own painful experiences, I've learned that when you take advice from people who don't know any more about the subject matter than you do, the quality of that advice is suspect. And the value is exactly what you paid for it…**NOTHING!**

I'm not saying that these are bad people. They are honest, intelligent, and they mean well. However, you must ask yourself, are these people the most qualified to give you advice?   Do they have any experience in what you are doing?

For some reason people love to offer advice on subjects they know nothing about. What puzzles me is how the recipients of this "*great wisdom*" listen to it and apply it without ever questioning the qualifications of those giving it.

I constantly get individuals who offer their "great wisdom" on the pitfalls of ebooks and they have never, I repeat **NEVER**, attempted to write one or even understand the process.

I kindly ask them where their information comes from, and they want to tell me, "my cousin said that it is not a good idea to write one". I politely say thank you and move on.

I guess if I would have listened to them you wouldn't be reading these words right now.
So, whom should you be listening to? I believe in taking advice only from those who are:

1) Qualified experts in their field and

2) Generating more money than I am in a specific area

These people are out there and they are accessible.

Don't be afraid to seek their help-even if you have to pay for it. I think you'll discover that if you pay for the opinion of a bona fide expert, the advice you receive will be more than worth the price and much better than the free advice from Cousin Jr.

The last "Hurdle" to Entrepreneurial Success that I

want to touch on is something I see so often. In fact I'm starting to lean towards this being the main culprit for the lack of success for entrepreneurs.

LACK OF FOCUS

When you have the entrepreneurial spirit you are always consciously or subconsciously looking for ways to make money. Believe me, there is nothing wrong with that.

The problem comes when you have too many things going on at the same time. You have so many things pulling you in so many directions that you can't get any of them running smoothly.

I am not saying that you can't do more than one thing at a time. In fact, many entrepreneurs find a way to do exactly that. I'm simply saying that it is difficult to start and run several businesses effectively.

I fell into this trap. Once you tap into the science of making money, so-called opportunities will start to flow from everywhere. I'm not saying that these are not viable opportunities. They just might not be viable for you at this time.

If I asked you if you knew of anyone who was involved in several different business ventures yet it seemed like they were continuously spinning their wheels, you would probably raise both hands.

In fact, this description might fit you.

All that I am saying is you may have to pause and take a look at your opportunities.

FOCUS on the business that gives the best opportunity, build the business, and put systems in place that can support the business then move on to other ventures.

With no focus you will never be able to hit the target that is designed for you.

Chapter 13

The Age of the Entrepreneur

The traditional wisdom of go to school; get a good education and get a good paying job with a good company is **DEAD.**

So much has changed from 30 to 40 years ago. Back then the corporations said, "We'll always be here and take care of you. Stay loyal to us and we will give you medical benefits and take care of your retirement."

Every year we have seen those promises vaporize. Over the last few years it has become common to read or hear that a company is **slashing** 10,000, 15,000, 30,000 jobs or **freezing** pensions or **forcing** their employees to be responsible for their own rising Health Care. The days of a safe, secure job are long gone.

Individuals have debated leaving their jobs and becoming entrepreneurs for decades. In the past, this debate focused on the opportunity and risk of going out on your own. Today, the real risk is staying with a company, because the job you perform could be permanently dismantled within a few years if not months.

I have several family members and friends who have spent the last few years under continuous stress, because they don't know what their future holds, with their job situation in limbo.

CORPORATE STRESS

The American Dream has become the American Nightmare. It has been reported that more and more people hate the very thought of going to work on Monday morning.

It has also been said that more suicides are committed on Monday morning before nine o'clock than at any other time of the week.

Today's employees can hardly wait for Friday to come around, and have developed a special cheer to celebrate it: **TGIF! Thank God It's Friday!**

Chapter 14

THE WORLD HAS CHANGED

There was a time when there were over 30 million farmers in America. Today it is less than 3 million. What happened to the rest of those farmers? They went into the manufacturing sector.

In the 1960s manufacturing was the bedrock of America's economic power. Over 40 percent of Americans worked in manufacturing.

Today, it is less than 20 percent.

You often hear about economic anguish caused by the emerging global society. <u>China, India, and other emerging countries</u> are taking away all the manufacturing jobs, and now the high tech and IT jobs are leaving.

The world is changing at a rapid pace. As human beings we have to live with an inherent paradox.

> *"The familiar comforts us, yet we are intrigued by the new."*

To survive we rely on constancy; but to grow we must embrace change.

Today, our basic relationship to change is itself changing. In the past, there was security in doing things the same way. Today the only security we have is embracing change.

And what is expediting the rapid change in the world? Technology!

Throughout history with the slow advancement of technology, an individual would be born and die without seeing any dramatic change in technology or their careers.

However, within the last 100 years or so the accelerated rate of technological change has been dramatic.

I want to point to one area of dramatic change to prove my point.

In 1985 there were several large manufacturing firms of vinyl records. By 1990-91 they were all closed down. CDs overtook the market in only 5 years.

And today we have an entire generation that doesn't know what a vinyl record is or what one looks like.

Now there is a new technology called MP3s or digital downloads that have captured a large share of the market. Now you can download MP3s from the Internet without buying CDs.

Look at what happened, it took 5 years to move from vinyl records to CDs and now you can download music with little physical material.

The point that I want to drive home is that the world is changing and changing fast. Changes that use to take place over 100 years or 75 years now happens in a few years and in some cases only a few months.

We have truly entered the Age of the Entrepreneur.

The Entrepreneur & Technology

When I speak of technology it is important to realize first and foremost I am speaking of personal skills.

Before you get drawn into the abyss of the **World Wide Web** you must understand that all of the changes that have occurred over the decades have happened <u>without violating the basic personal skills of individuals</u>.

First, your basic skills must be intact. The ability to read, write, speak, calculate and process information is the core skillsets that everyone needs in any type of job and business.

Secondly, specialized skills that you have learned up to this point come into play. It used to be very smart to learn a specialized skill and master that skill. Once you mastered a special skill you had a job or career for life.

Today, relying on a specialized skill is business suicide, because areas where you specialize transforms and sometimes disappear in a couple of years.

You should analyze your specialized skill and see what unique experiences it brings with it, and draw on those experiences to see how you can take that skill and go further in your endeavors.

The single most important skill set for an entrepreneur today is *"having the ability to learn new things"*, being able to adapt. Your competitive advantage and your capacity to generate and create wealth will depend on how fast and how well you learn something new.

The Internet

The Internet is the single most powerful force driving the growth and transformation of today's economy. There are hundreds of millions of people using the Internet.

Throughout history one of the critical factors in economic expansion has been the building of roads, the railroads and the highways. They have always served to move both "information exchange" and "free trade".

Look at the term used to describe the Internet "*information super-highway*". The Internet is a new highway system and has knocked down previous barriers to trade and communication.

The capacity for an Entrepreneur to grow is now 100 fold. You can literally create a product or service in your basement and sell it instantaneously all over the world.

Whatever area or field you choose to apply your entrepreneurial energy, the Internet is your most important technology.

The Internet is the only medium where you can communicate, find a new product, find new resources, tell your existing customers about products or services, research new fields, learn new knowledge and new skills right at your fingertips.

OTHER TECHNOLOGY

It doesn't matter if you have an appliance store or a high-tech firm, your business will do much better if you take advantage of technology.

When you look at today's business environment, staying on top of cutting edge technology cannot be stressed enough.
Podcasting, audio, video conferencing, web conferencing, blogs, conference calls, membership sites, newsletters, video streaming and distribution, Discussion Groups or Forums all add to the effectiveness and efficiency of your business.

All of these technologies and more are to help you with your most valuable resource: **YOUR TIME!**

There is nothing you can do to add more hours in a day. However, you can choose how you use those hours.

The most important aspect of technology, particularly the Internet, is it is an **instant global communication system** and your ability to use the Internet and technology to leverage your time...it is critical to your success.

Chapter 15

THE TECHNOLOGICAL EDGE

In the mid 1970s, only the large corporations had the biggest and best technology and computers available.

Back then and throughout the '80s the only way to have access to the best technology was to be involved with or employed by these large corporations.

Today, the complete opposite is true. You may find the latest and best in your pocket or held in your hand. I mentioned the number of mobile devices and tablets earlier.

This gives the entrepreneur a tremendous edge over the large corporation. Technology is changing faster than ever, and a large organization has an enormous challenge bringing in and integrating new technology.

Today, technology is geared toward a fast-moving, highly adaptable business climate based on personal one on one transaction.

It is no longer smart or economical to make one model of anything and force everyone to use it. Dell Computers proved that.

The greatest opportunities are not to go work for a large corporation, but to go into business for you.

Technology makes it possible to become **Financially Independent** practically overnight.

Entrepreneurs Go Where Growth Is

When I spoke with the great Dennis Kimbro, the best-selling author of *Think and Grow Rich: A Black Choice* we discussed how black people don't even consider entrepreneurship as a viable career option.

And those who do choose to start a business usually enter as "mom & pop" operations just to keep a *"roof over their heads and get the clothes out of the cleaners."*

Very rarely do we start businesses to grow enormous enterprises. It still amazes me that when we talk of starting a business, our choices are limited.

We talk of barbershops, beauty salons, car washes, cleaners, and dollar stores. Recently we have ventured into Real Estate and Real Estate related areas.

All of these are good businesses and can be very successful if structured and marketed properly. However, the opportunity to get involved in new and Emerging Industries have never been greater.

The greatest fortunes to be made in the future will not be made in what people were doing five, 10 or 15 years ago. The fortunes will be made in industries that barely exist today.

If you go into an existing industry, as an entrepreneur, you are going to be working harder. Putting in more hours and working harder to beat the competition, because there are mature entrepreneurs already present.

That's not necessarily a bad thing, but you must be

aware. Every entrepreneur knows the idea is to work smarter not harder.

If you go into a new or emerging industry with this idea in mind you become the one distributing or supplying the new product or service that will be in demand.

The key is you have to be alert to see what is new and emerging, because once everyone else has taken notice to that industry it is no longer new and emerging.

The bottom line is that with technology and the Internet in particular, you have the ability to be on the cutting edge of new and exciting things.

The challenge is to train yourself to be alert to see and act in the 'New Economy'.

Chapter 16

Entrepreneurs in The Age of Connectivity

In the Age of Connectivity, all it takes is information or ideas and a way to market them to become financially independent and possibly wealthy.

It is possible for individuals who are off the radar of wealth one year to be very wealthy the next.

In the **Agrarian Age**, only those who owned large tracks of fertile agricultural land were considered the rich. During this era you could become wealthy by controlling the land, steel, grain, cattle, or other critical physical staples.

Those who controlled the transportation and distribution of those resources also gained great wealth.

This era produced what is known as the **"resource millionaires"**.

In the **Industrial Age**, wealth shifted from the agricultural land to real estate or rocky land. Rocky land became more valuable than fertile land.

On the rocky land buildings, factories, warehouses, and residential homes could be built.

Unlike the Agrarian Age, you did not have to be of noble birth to become rich and powerful in this era.

In the Industrial Age, entrepreneurs started with nothing

and became billionaires.

This is the age that gave birth to Henry Ford and the automobile industry. You may also recognize the names of Rockefeller, Stanford, and Carnegie.

This age also provided great opportunity for the pioneers, innovators and masters of manufacturing. A large number of people became millionaires by finding cheaper ways of making things by using new materials like plastic and by shipping production overseas.

This era produced what is known as the "**manufacturing millionaires**".

It was in the Industrial Age that the idea of "*go to school so you can find a good job*" became popular.

You went to school; got the one job for life, worked your way up the corporate ladder or union ladder, and when you retired, the company and the government took care of you for the rest of your life.
Needless to say, that era is **DEAD**!

As I mentioned earlier, in the 'Age of Connectivity', it takes information or ideas and **a way to market them** and you can become wealthy.

The World Wide Web has changed the rules for anyone wanting to become an Entrepreneur and wanting to become wealthy.

I once heard a saying, "Money is an idea".

The better you get at nurturing and growing your ideas

the easier it will become to turn your ideas into money. And you'll begin to see the reality that it doesn't take money to make money, it takes ideas.

The challenge is breaking the "**old ideas**" of the Industrial Age.

BUSINESS IS MARKETING

This is where I get tremendous resistance. Everyone wants to talk about how his or her product or service is better than someone else's product or service. And that may be true, but who knows that.

It doesn't matter if you do have the best product or service, *if you can't convince the market that you have the better product or service, you're dead.*

There are warehouses full of products all over the world. There are products sitting on shelves for months at a time.

Most entrepreneurs fail miserably at advertising and marketing their products or services. *Large amounts of money and opportunities are lost because entrepreneurs try to mimic what major corporations are doing.*

In the 'Age of Connectivity' **you must become a master at marketing and connecting**. Just as this new economy has empowered the entrepreneur, it has also empowered the consumer.

Customers can take their time to seek out the product or service of their choosing. You have to have the ability to create a message that will compel them to choose you over other products or services just like yours.

You may currently have a product or service now that you can't seem to sell. You must find a way to educate your customer about your product or service.

That's the power of the 'Age of Connectivity'. It has never been easier to target your market and deliver your message directly to them and educate them about you and your product.

Marketing Expanded

I just gave you the key to business success in the 21st century and beyond. I want to repeat it to give it clarity.

There are two aspects to every business. To understand this most important point, puts you in a league of your own.

Every business has its core expertise, the product or service that business provides. This is where 99% of the business owners or entrepreneurs stop.

If you ask what business they are in, they'll say, *"I'm in the design business"* or *"I'm in the plumbing business"* or *"I'm in the real estate business"*. This is just one aspect.

The other aspect or what I like to call the real business that any businessperson is in is the marketing business.

The real estate, the plumbing, the designing, the insurance, etc… these are the "vehicles" that you choose to do business in.

As an entrepreneur you choose one of these "vehicles" to make money in.

Just as a side bar, if you are not in business to make money you will not be in business long.

Now back to my main point, as I said earlier, "Business is Marketing". Without marketing you have no productive activity. **There is no income**.

You just have a product in a warehouse, basement, or a garage, or a skill or service sitting idle in an individual or company.

When you understand this simple fact that your business is not the product or service itself, but that your business is really in letting the people that might be interested in your product or service know that you have those products, at a high value, and these products can make their lives immediately better when they get them.

When you do that you've got it. That's what we call Marketing!

Chapter 17

The Key to Success in the Age of Connectivity

As we get close to ending this book I am going to give you the key to success in this exciting Age of Connectivity.

If you can wrap your mind around what I'm about to share with you, you will be able to capitalize on all of the mega trends and technologies that we touched on earlier.

You see it doesn't matter how great your product is or how great your story and messaging is, it doesn't matter how gifted you are and how committed you are to your mission

You need a large enough mass of people who know you exist. You need a group of people who care about you and what you have to say, you need a... **viable platform.**

You may be asking, *"What is a Platform?"*

Simply stated, your platform is a combination of your knowledge, your voice, your unique experience and expertise and who knows you and is willing to pay to hear you speak or purchase your books, products, and services.

Your platform is your **NETWORK,** Your platform is your **LIST** of **Clients**, **Customers**, and **Subscribers** Your platform is your **ABILITY** to **DRAW ATTENTION** and **CREATE BUZZ** Your platform is your **SUITE** of

PRODUCTS and **SERVICES** Your platform is your **POSITIONING** in the **MARKETPLACE**

You need a platform today. Every business needs a platform. Everyone needs a platform.

I think people sense this anyway; look at all of the people opening up accounts on Facebook, Twitter, Youtube, Linkedin, Intstagram, etc…

Most just don't know that they are trying to develop a platform, all they know is that they have something to say and they want to get their message and voice out.

Most don't know that with a platform they can create their own financial freedom. If you use your platform properly you can get paid what you're truly worth.

A properly constructed platform gives you the ability to get in the media and featured on important websites and blogs. You will have the ability to access powerful Joint Ventures and Strategic Alliances.

This makes promoting and marketing your products and services easier and more powerful.

A properly constructed platform is TRUE LEVERAGE and TRUE WEALTH that could pay you for life.

Let me give you a couple of examples of what I'm talking about…

Any small business without customers is going to go out of business, but let's just look at a restaurant. Without a flow of customers the restaurant will be closed for good, but with a well-constructed platform the owner could send out an email blast, text message, tweet, post to Facebook or YouTube video and drive customers into the restaurant within hours.

If done correctly, this could be done daily, weekly, monthly and for years far off into the future.

A struggling author has an excellent message that could change a lot of lives, but no platform. With a well-constructed platform she could sell a few thousand books in a few weeks to a month. That's enough to become an Amazon best-seller, in fact that's enough to become a New York Times bestselling author.

You have a Lawyer struggling to get clients, again no platform. If she had one she could have a waiting list of prospective clients. At that point fees are not even issue.

Being able to drive customers through your doors at will, selling thousands of books and becoming a bestseller, or having clients waiting to pay you the fees you command are easy when you
have a platform.

And do you want to know the really cool part?

In the past, in order to properly construct a platform, you needed an agent, a publicist, a publisher, years of exposure, and thousands of dollars.

Today you can do most of the things necessary to begin building a powerful, lasting, and profitable platform for free with the right focus and effort.
You should start today!

We're right at the end, but there is one more skill that I must reinforce before we close this book. I've touched on it earlier, but I wanted to focus on it here because if you master this skill and properly construct a platform your business and entrepreneurial life will be secure forever.

Here it is…

Chapter 18

The Most Important Skill in the Age Of Connectivity

I'll go straight to the point here!

The most important skill that you are going to need in the "Age of Connectivity" is networking and building effective relationships.

That may seem oxymoronic considering that with technology and the different platforms like FaceBook and Twitter you don't have to see someone face to face.

However, with the advances in technology it has also made it faster and easier for your flaws to be exposed. It's easier to offend someone whether intentional or not intentional and leave a lasting digital record of it.

Also, with this advancement the barrier to entry into the marketplace is lowered. This has allowed the crooks and predators to enter and wreak havoc and destroy lives so much so that we live in a culture of low trust.

The only way to restore trust is with proper networking and building effective relationships.

I know you probably have some reservations in your mind about networking based upon what you think networking is.

But I'll tell you this... If you're going to achieve **any** degree of success, whether it is finding a job, finding more customers, finding opportunities, or finding profitable contacts, you are going to have to network.

If you are going to build a business anywhere in the world you will have to network, you will have to know people, you will have to build relationships, you will have to nurture and grow those relationships into your own group of powerful contacts.

The success you desire…

Can't be done with out it!

I know that hearing the word Networking conjures up images in your mind.

Images like being at a bar or a cocktail party and having to approach someone cold and saying, "Hi my name is Mike and I would like to talk to you."

Or

Finding the CEO of a company and attempting to give her your 3 min. elevator pitch.

Or

You having to be this suave, smooth talking person with the ability to get everyone to like you.

And I can understand why those images come up… that's what we see on TV or someone who doesn't have a clue said that this is how Networking should be done.

The truth is there aren't too many qualified teachers of effective Networking and building effective relationships.

In fact, Networking is an entire course of study and we don't have the time or space to cover it here.

But I would strongly recommend that you get your hands on everything my mentor and friend George Fraser has on the subject.

He is literally the father of modern Networking amongst Black People and one of the top experts in the world on the subject.

Networking leads you to...

Joint Ventures & Strategic Alliances

'Age of Connectivity' entrepreneurs understand **OPR** (Other People's Resources) and **OPC** (Other Peoples Customers). The idea of working cooperatively for mutual profit and benefit with other entrepreneurs excites the new entrepreneur.

One of the best things an entrepreneur can do is to partner with a larger company or other like minded entrepreneurs to share valuable resources.

You can achieve explosive growth in your market if you have access to either JVs or Alliance partners that will introduce you to their customers or potential clients with their endorsement.

You may ask why someone would introduce you to

their customers or other key contacts. Well, the smart entrepreneur knows that in order to keep their customers satisfied they have to continue to introduce them to new and better products and services.

That is why in the last section we stressed the need to construct your own powerful platform. Having a platform increases the desire in others to want to partner and work with you.

It is only the '**Old Economy'** entrepreneurs who are so competition freaked out that they will not do what's best for them and their customers.

You see without Joint Ventures and Strategic Alliances you can't expand your customer base. *It will remain limited by your own client acquisition techniques*.

So if you get nothing else from reading these few pages, you should know that in the 'Age of Connectivity' you're just one Joint Venture or Strategic Alliance Partner away from being wealthy.

Make it a priority to learn how to **Network** and construct **Joint Ventures** and **Strategic Alliances, the 'Currency' of the 'Age of Connectivity'**.

Chapter 19

Entrepreneurs Take Action

The last point I want to leave you with is crucial to your success.

"Nothing Happens until Something Moves"

No matter what information you have received in this book or any other book for that matter, it is useless if you don't take action.

I hope by reading these words you have come to the conclusion that there is ample opportunity for you to be a successful entrepreneur.

The time has never been better and the resources have never been more accessible.

It is up to you to take action to escape your self-imposed prison.

It is up to you to take action to take control of your life.

It is up to you to take action to find the knowledge and know how you need.

It is up to you to take action to shed old baggage and discover new fresh capabilities.

It is up to you to take action to generate the income you deserve.

It is up to you to take action to surround yourself with positive well-meaning people.

It is up to you to take action to promote you, your ideas, your business, your products and services.

It is up to you to take action to turn apparent failure into success.

I Hope and Pray that I have done my part in helping you on your entrepreneurial journey, the rest is up to you.

But just in case I'll be here.

Chapter 20

My Closing Thoughts

I know that this is not a **'Magic Bullet'** or a **'Secret Blueprint'** to succeeding as an entrepreneur in the "Age of Connectivity'.

In fact, they don't exist. And if anyone tells you that they have the whole concept of entrepreneurship nailed down to a couple of pages…**RUN!**

As I mentioned earlier **'Black Entrepreneurship'** is very important in this **'New Era'**.

The Black community that we love will only be able to give our children and our children's children what they need if we lay the foundation for them.

The housing, the food, the clothing, the schooling, the parks, the jobs, the peace, the Dreams, the Equality, the Justice, the Freedom…

….they shouldn't have to **BEG** for this and neither should you!

There are 3 things that will help you ensure your success as an entrepreneur.

1) You must continue your education and training on entrepreneurship
2) You must be able get to the resources you need to grow and sustain your business
3) You must connect with other entrepreneurs who can support you and encourage you.

Can't wait to see and hear of your Victories and Successes!

Bro. Bedford

www.ingramcontent.com/pod-product-compliance
Lightning Source LLC
Chambersburg PA
CBHW051734170526
45167CB00002B/927